SWEET AROMA

Sweet Aroma
The Fragrance of the Firstborn

H.L. ROBERTSON

Sweet Aroma
Copyright © 2016 by H. L. Robertson. All rights reserved.

No part of this publication may be reproduced, stored in a retrieval system or transmitted in any way by any means, electronic, mechanical, photocopy, recording or otherwise without the prior permission of the author except as provided by USA copyright law.

Scripture quotations marked (KJV) are taken from the *Holy Bible, King James Version, Cambridge*, 1769. Used by permission. All rights reserved.

Fairhaven Media, Lynchburg, TN

Cover design by Joana Quilantang
Interior design by Jomar Ouano

Published in the United States of America
ISBN: 978-0-9987480-6-1

Religion / Christian Life / Spiritual Growth

16.01.27

To my dad, who is now in glory,
for modeling what a Bible teacher ought to be

Contents

Introduction 9

1 Words 11
2 People, Places, and Things 17
3 The Past 23
4 The Present 29
5 The Future 35
6 Pray without Ceasing 41
7 Enter the Temple 49
8 Get Dressed 55
9 The Prodigal 63

Appendix A: Prayers 71
Appendix B: Prayers for "Entering In" 75

Introduction

Several years ago, the Lord gave me a sermon entitled "What Does God Smell." That message, the study it required, and the subsequent revelations concerning this topic were the basis for a stunning change in my understanding of how we relate to God and how He perceives us. Second Corinthians says,

> Now thanks be unto God, which always causeth us to triumph in Christ, and maketh manifest the savour of his knowledge by us in every place. For we are unto God a sweet savour of Christ, in them that are saved, and in them that perish: To the one we are the savour of death unto death; and to the other the savour of life unto life. (2 Cor. 2:14–16)

As I read these scriptures and others like it, I began to realize not only the tremendous number of references to smell in the Bible but the deep significance of those passages. It seems that God has a very sensitive olfactory sense! His perception of the sacrifices offered to Him and the people making the sacrifices were very closely tied to, literally, what they smelled like spiritually. I then began to realize that there was a very positive side to these principles of "sweet savour" that we as Christians can operate in to enter into a deeper and more freely expressed relationship with Father God.

In the ensuing chapters, I would like to pursue this study from, first, a historical perspective, examining the nation of Israel and their spiritual "aroma." Then, I want to look at a contemporary perspective in relation to our lives and how we might "smell" to God. Hopefully, we will learn what this means for our relationship to Him and how we can better implement a lifestyle of sweet aroma before our creator. Lastly, I will challenge us to proactively seek to look, feel, and smell more and more like the "firstborn."

1

Words

In any in-depth study of God's Word, there eventually comes into play a centuries-long principle regarding the interpretation of Scripture. This is called the law of first mention. Simply put, the first time a particular subject or concept is mentioned in Scripture, it is accorded special significance. This is because studies have shown consistently that the first time a concept appears in the Bible, there is a special and often times hidden or veiled meaning, and an added weight of importance connected with that particular verse or verses. The first mention will, for instance, often introduce an important doctrinal truth that had up to that point in biblical history been unknown or unrecognized.

The first mention of the idea of a sweet aroma, or as KJV renders it, sweet savour, is found in Genesis 8 in a description of Noah's sacrifice after leaving the ark.

> And Noah builded an altar unto the LORD; and took of every clean beast, and of every clean fowl, and offered burnt offerings on the altar. And the LORD smelled a sweet savour; and the LORD said in his heart, I will not again curse the ground any more for man's sake; for the imagination of man's heart is evil from his youth; neither will I again smite any more every thing living, as I have done. (Gen. 8:20–21)

Here, we see the first mention of an important concept: the idea that God is temporarily pacified in his anger at men's sins by a sacrifice that produces what Scripture describes as a sweet aroma. The Hebrew words used in this passage are *niychoach reyach*. *Niychoach* is a word which means to sooth or to tranquilize. *Reyach* is a derivative of the word *ruach* (smell or odor), from which we get a slightly different, and vastly important, word also transliterated *ruach*, which means spirit, breath, or wind. It is this word which is used in the phrase describing God's Spirit: *ruach ha kodesh* or Holy Spirit. Thus, the phrase *niychoach reyach* can literally be translated an "odor of soothing" and is closely related to the wording and concept of the Spirit. In this way, this phrase gives us a picture of the idea of a sacrifice changing the spiritual atmosphere before God Almighty from that of seeing and smelling our fallen sinfulness to one of a pleasing smell produced by a sacrifice for that sinfulness.

This is the introduction of a very important concept. For example, in Exodus 29, we find this description:

> And thou shalt burn the whole ram upon the altar: it is a burnt offering unto the LORD: it is a sweet savour, an offering made by fire unto the LORD. And thou shalt receive them of their hands, and burn them upon the altar for a burnt offering, for a sweet savour before the LORD: it is an offering made by fire unto the LORD. (Exod. 29:18, 25)

This verse describes a particular type of burnt offering which was intended to be an aroma of soothing to the Lord. We also see this type of description in Ezekiel:

> For in mine holy mountain, in the mountain of the height of Israel, saith the Lord God, there shall all the house of Israel, all of them in the land, serve me: there will I accept them, and there will I require your offerings, and the firstfruits of your oblations, with all your holy things. I will accept you with your sweet savour, when I bring you out from the people, and gather you out of the countries wherein ye have been scattered; and I will be sanctified in you before the heathen. And ye shall know that I am the LORD. (Ezek. 20:40–42)

This Hebrew phrase is used in the Old Testament sixty-one times, thirty-nine in the Torah alone, and in forty-one of those uses, it is referring to a sacrifice to God. Any word picture shown to us that many times in so concentrated a group of scriptures surely has a special significance of great importance.

Old Testament scriptures portray the negative picture of this idea as well. Leviticus shows us the "flip side" to this principle: "And I will make your cities waste, and bring your sanctuaries unto desolation, and I will not smell the savour of your sweet odours" (Lev. 26:31).

In other words, if the Israelites worshipped idols and were rebellious, God didn't smell the sweet and soothing aroma of their sacrifices, and thus, he maintained his anger and wrath against them. Biblical history tells us that this scenario played out literally for centuries in the times of the kings and later during the various captivities and dispersions. The nation would rebel against God in some significant way. This would arouse God's anger against them. This in turn would bring about defeat, oppression, and, ultimately, captivity and slavery. The nation would then repent and seek God, who in his great love and mercy would forgive them and send them a deliverer who would defeat their enemies and set them free. This vicious cycle of rebellion and repentance was repeated for over a thousand years until the horrific events of 70 AD, in which the Roman tenth legion razed Jerusalem to the ground and proceeded to build a pagan city named Aelia Capitolina dedicated in honor of Zeus. This final, and at the time, seemingly irrevocable judgment brought down the curtain on a millennium of God's wrath that went unmitigated by these "sweet aromas."

In Isaiah's prophecy, we are presented with a clear and concise description of the actual workings of this principle:

> I have spread out my hands all the day unto a rebellious people, which walketh in a way that was not good, after their own thoughts; A people that provoketh me to anger continually to my face; that sacrificeth in gardens, and burneth incense upon altars of brick; Which remain among the graves, and lodge in the monuments, which eat swine's flesh, and broth of abominable things is in their vessels; Which say, Stand by thyself, come not near to me; for I am holier than thou. These are a smoke in my nose, a fire that burneth all the day. (Isa. 65:2–5)

Notice the description beginning in verse 2: "a rebellious people" who "provoke me to anger." Now, read the next phrase: "to my face." This is the Hebrew word *paniym*, which means simply face or countenance. This shows us a view of these sinful acts being literally, as we would say, "in his face." He then proceeds to enumerate the idolatrous abominations they are committing and concludes with the words "These are a smoke in my nose." This Hebrew word is *aph*. It is very interesting that this particular word can on one hand be translated face, nose, or nostrils, or on the other hand, it can also be rendered anger or wrath. Here, we have a tremendous picture of the stench of their sins coming up not only before his face but into his nose! The stench in turn produces a violent reaction. God says in verse 6, "I will not keep silence, but will recompense, even recompense into their bosom" (Isa. 65:6).

Finally, we see this same principle at work in a New Testament example. In Acts 10, we find a picture of good works coming up before God:

> There was a certain man in Caesarea called Cornelius, a centurion of the band called the Italian band, A devout man, and one that feared God with all his house, which gave much alms to the people, and prayed to God always. He saw in a vision evidently about the ninth hour of the day an angel of God coming in to him, and saying unto him, Cornelius. And when he looked on him, he was afraid, and said, What is it, Lord? And he said unto him, Thy prayers and thine alms are come up for a memorial before God. (Acts 10:1–4)

These verses depict a situation in which Cornelius's righteous acts of charity "come up for a memorial before God." Although the sweet aroma is not mentioned specifically, the concept is clearly understood to be in operation by the wording used: "come up…before."

2

People, Places, and Things

Genesis 3 gives us the narrative of the fall of man. Found in this passage is the first usage of the Hebrew noun *paniym* (face) to describe a face in anthropomorphic or human terms. The only previous uses are related to the "face of the ground" or the "face of the earth." It is used here of the face of the Almighty.

> Now the serpent was more subtil than any beast of the field which the LORD God had made. And he said unto the woman, Yea, hath God said, Ye shall not eat of every tree of the garden? And the woman said unto the serpent, We may eat of the fruit of the trees of the garden: But of the fruit of the tree which is in the midst of the garden, God hath said, Ye shall not eat of it, neither shall ye touch it, lest ye die. And the serpent said unto the woman, Ye shall not surely die: For God doth know that in the

day ye eat thereof, then your eyes shall be opened, and ye shall be as gods, knowing good and evil. And when the woman saw that the tree was good for food, and that it was pleasant to the eyes, and a tree to be desired to make one wise, she took of the fruit thereof, and did eat, and gave also unto her husband with her; and he did eat. And the eyes of them both were opened, and they knew that they were naked; and they sewed fig leaves together, and made themselves aprons. And they heard the voice of the LORD God walking in the garden in the cool of the day: and Adam and his wife hid themselves from the presence of the LORD God amongst the trees of the garden. (Gen. 3:2–8)

Here again is an occasion for employing the law of first mention. Adam and Eve are said to be hiding themselves from the presence, literally the *paniym* or face of God. The question begs to be asked: did they instinctively know that their sin and rebellion cause them to stink in the nostrils of God? The words used to describe the scene suggest that they did. Verse 8 says that God came in the "cool of the day." The word translated "cool" is *ruach*, which means breath, wind, or spirit and is derived as shown in chapter 1 from another word transliterated as *ruach*, which means blow or smell—literally the blowing or sniffing of the nostrils. Armed with this knowledge, the picture here becomes clear: God comes in the fragrant twilight time only to find that the normal evening aromas have been replaced by the stench of sin. He immediately calls to them, but they have hidden themselves in a unique place: the tree of knowledge itself! The Hebrew phrase translated "amongst the trees" could be more accurately rendered "within the tree." The Hebrew word for "tree" is singular in this case. It is very difficult to maintain a logical sentence construction based on "among the tree." Moreover, the word for *amongst*, *tavek*, is translated "within" twenty times in the Old Testament. This gives a much more natural "within the tree." It appears that they hid within the very tree that caused their downfall. God is seeking to regain the relationship they have enjoyed up to this point, but they allow their shame to drive them away from him. How deep is the human trait of denial that we often plunge into the very thing that is destroying us in order to hide our guilt, all the while isolating ourselves from a loving creator who is seeking diligently to restore us to fellowship.

In chapter 1, we looked at the story of Noah building the altar after the ark landed and the implications of the law of first mention as applies to that event. Now we need to examine the same story again from the viewpoint of God. He says in Genesis 6,

> And GOD saw that the wickedness of man was great in the earth, and that every imagination of the thoughts of his heart was only evil continually. And it repented the Lord that he had made man on

> the earth, and it grieved him at his heart. And the LORD said, I will destroy man whom I have created from the face of the earth; both man, and beast, and the creeping thing, and the fowls of the air; for it repenteth me that I have made them. (Gen. 6:6–7)

Notice that he says "every imagination of the thoughts of his heart was only evil continually." In fact, he cites this as one of the primary reasons he is destroying all mankind except the immediate family of Noah. Now take another look at the Genesis 8 text:

> And the LORD smelled a sweet savour; and the LORD said in his heart, I will not again curse the ground any more for man's sake; for the imagination of man's heart is evil from his youth; neither will I again smite any more every thing living, as I have done. (Gen. 8: 21)

Notice the almost identical wording of the two passages: both say that the imaginations of their hearts are evil. In the first set of verses, God sets about to destroy mankind for this reason. Then in the second passage, he states in a covenant promise that he will not destroy all living things again, even though he reiterates the statement concerning their thoughts being evil. The difference? Notice the first statement in verse 21: "And the LORD smelled a sweet savour…" (Gen. 8:21).

That one act of sacrifice by Noah caused a pleasing aroma to rise up before God, soothing his wrath. The spiritual condition of the people involved seems remarkably similar, yet the act of sacrifice produced the sweet savor that dramatically changed the outcome.

In Genesis 19, a similar but localized judgment is pronounced by God for Sodom's and Gomorrah's sinful behavior.

> And there came two angels to Sodom at even; and Lot sat in the gate of Sodom: and Lot seeing them rose up to meet them; and he bowed himself with his face toward the ground; And the men said unto Lot, Hast thou here any besides? son in law, and thy sons, and thy daughters, and whatsoever thou hast in the city, bring them out of this place: For we will destroy this place, because the cry of them is waxen great before the face of the LORD; and the LORD hath sent us to destroy it. (Gen. 19:1, 12–13)

Once again, the Bible records an instance man's sin coming up before God: "the cry…is great before the face [paniym] of the Lord." As in the case of Noah, God spares those who are righteous before meting out judgment. In fact, this is a continuing theme throughout the Old Testament as God repeatedly told his followers to make a sacrifice of a soothing aroma. There are no less than thirty-seven times that Moses is instructed by the Lord to make an offering of a "sweet savour"—*niychoach reyach*—in the Torah. Through these scriptures, we begin to see the vital importance God places on this spiritual principle.

3

The Past

As we have seen in the previous chapters, the sense of smell is very important to the Lord. It is a harbinger of how we will be reacted to and received by God. In fact, every step of the Old Testament temple worship had an odor or aroma associated with it. Each station was not only appointed for a particular part of the sacrificial system but was also playing a vital role in covering the sin nature of the priest as he made his way through the process.

The first station the priest encountered was the laver. Its purpose is obvious; it was used for washing by the priests before they ministered in the temple: "And Aaron and his sons thou shalt bring unto the door of the tabernacle of the congregation, and shalt wash them with water" (Exod. 29:4).

Next came the altar of burnt offerings. Here, the priests handled the animal sacrifices, burned them in the fire, and sprinkled their blood on the altar, pouring the rest at the base of the altar.

> And he shall lay his hand upon the head of his offering, and kill it at the door of the tabernacle of the congregation: and Aaron's sons the priests shall sprinkle the blood upon the altar round about. And he shall offer of the sacrifice of the peace offering an offering made by fire unto the LORD; the fat that covereth the inwards, and all the fat that is upon the inwards, And the two kidneys, and the fat that is on them, which is by the flanks, and the caul above the liver, with the kidneys, it shall he take away. And Aaron's sons shall burn it on the altar upon the burnt sacrifice, which is upon the wood that is on the fire: it is an offering made by fire, of a sweet savour unto the LORD. (Lev. 3:3–5)

The offerings were also sprinkled with salt:

> And every oblation of thy meat offering shalt thou season with salt; neither shalt thou suffer the salt of the covenant of thy God to be lacking from thy meat offering: with all thine offerings thou shalt offer salt. (Lev. 2:13)

> All the heave offerings of the holy things, which the children of Israel offer unto the LORD, have I given

thee, and thy sons and thy daughters with thee, by a statute for ever: it is a covenant of salt for ever before the LORD unto thee and to thy seed with thee. (Num. 18:19)

When the priest finished the sacrifice in preparation for entering the holy place, he had been washed, covered in the smell of cattle, wreathed in smoke, and drenched with animal blood. Everything about this process is filled with odors and smells. The work of covering his fallenness was well underway.

The priest now enters the holy place. Inside this section of the temple, he places the freshly baked shewbread on the table. According to rabbinical tradition, each loaf had a lump of frankincense on it: "And upon the table of shewbread they shall spread a cloth of blue, and put thereon the dishes, and the spoons, and the bowls, and covers to cover withal: and the continual bread shall be thereon" (Num. 4:7).

He then tends the menorah, cleaning it, trimming its wicks, and filling it with olive oil: "The pure candlestick, with the lamps thereof, even with the lamps to be set in order, and all the vessels thereof, and the oil for light, And the golden altar, and the anointing oil, and the sweet incense, and the hanging for the tabernacle door" (Exod. 39:37–38).

Finally, he sprinkles blood on the altar of incense along with coals of fire from the great altar and the holy incense:

"And the priest shall put some of the blood upon the horns of the altar of sweet incense before the LORD, which is in the tabernacle of the congregation" (Lev. 4:7).

And again, "And he put the golden altar in the tent of the congregation before the vail: And he burnt sweet incense thereon; as the LORD commanded Moses" (Exod. 40:27).

The following quote from my book *Into His Presence* (2013) describes this incense:

> This incense was made of equal parts of stacte, a sweet spice probably derived from the storax tree; onycha, a strong scent made from ground mussel shells; galbanum, a strong, disagreeable smelling aromatic gum; and frankincense, a fragrant gum made from the boswellia tree. These ingredients combined to produce a formidable incense which, since its recipe was formulated by God himself, was no doubt, a "soothing aroma" to the Lord.

Again, the whole process of the ministry within the holy place surrounds and permeates the priest with aromas: the bread, the frankincense, the olive oil, the blood, the fire, and the incense. Before the high priest went into the holy of holies (again, with blood, fire, and incense), he was completely clothed in sweet aromas. This clothing was absolutely necessary. If the high priest entered the holiest without it, he would be killed instantly. God simply cannot countenance our sin nature in his holy presence. In Leviticus 16, we are told specifically that the cloud of incense covering the mercy seat on the ark was essential so that he would "die not."

> And Aaron shall bring the bullock of the sin offering, which is for himself, and shall make an atonement for himself, and for his house, and shall kill the bullock of the sin offering which is for himself: And he shall take a censer full of burning coals of fire from off the altar before the LORD, and his hands full of sweet incense beaten small, and bring it within the vail: And he shall put the incense upon the fire before the LORD, that the cloud of the incense may cover the mercy seat that is upon the testimony, that he die not: And he shall take of the blood of the bullock, and sprinkle it with his finger upon the mercy seat eastward; and before the mercy seat shall he sprinkle of the blood with his finger seven times. (Lev. 16:12–14)

The need for this covering didn't begin here in the temple; it is seen all the way back at the fall. In the Genesis 3 narrative, we see that once Adam's and Eve's eyes are opened, they instinctively know that they need a covering.

> And the eyes of them both were opened, and they knew that they were naked; and they sewed fig leaves together, and made themselves aprons. And

> they heard the voice of the LORD God walking in the garden in the cool of the day: and Adam and his wife hid themselves from the presence of the LORD God amongst the trees of the garden. And the LORD God called unto Adam, and said unto him, Where art thou? And he said, I heard thy voice in the garden, and I was afraid, because I was naked; and I hid myself. And he said, Who told thee that thou wast naked? Hast thou eaten of the tree, whereof I commanded thee that thou shouldest not eat? (Gen. 3:7–11)

Little did they realize that their sin had robbed them of the covering of God's glory they had previously been robed in. All through history, man has been on a futile quest to restore that covering. In the following chapters, we will see that God himself has intervened to do just that.

4

The Present

As the previous chapter points out, mankind has been seeking to regain the glory and covering lost in the garden. Adam's and Eve's fig leaf coverings were insufficient, even as a temporary measure. The fall had left them utterly bankrupt spiritually, and God stepped in to make the first blood sacrifice by killing animals and using their skins to make them clothes: "Unto Adam also and to his wife did the Lord God make coats of skins, and clothed them" (Gen. 3:21).

Little did they know how insufficient their attempt to cover themselves had been. The leaves would have simply withered, and their problem would have continued. Any human attempt to establish the covering of righteousness will be as futile as theirs was: "But we are all as an unclean thing, and all our righteousnesses are as filthy rags; and we all do fade as a leaf; and our iniquities, like the wind, have taken us away" (Isa. 64:6).

Notice the reference to a "leaf." Here, Isaiah is telling us plainly that all human effort to cover our fallen sinfulness will meet with the same utter failure as Adam and Eve's. These man-made coverings may appear sufficient or even good for a short time, but ultimately, they will "fade as a leaf."

Just as God had to step in and physically cover Adam and Eve, he also stepped in through Jesus's death on the cross to provide a spiritual covering.

> I will greatly rejoice in the LORD, my soul shall be joyful in my God; for he hath clothed me with the garments of salvation, he hath covered me with the robe of righteousness, as a bridegroom decketh himself with ornaments, and as a bride adorneth herself with her jewels. (Isa. 61:10)

Notice that there are "garments of salvation" and a "robe of righteousness." The first is a garment to cover our spiritual nakedness just as God made clothing for Adam and Eve. The second is a covering that spiritually restores the glory of righteousness lost at the foot of the tree of knowledge. This time, however, it is His blood that was shed—His sacrifice that was required to make these clothes. Salvation provides not only Christ *in* us but also Christ *on* us. As Isaiah pointed out, our righteousness is filth in the sight of God. Jesus told the Pharisees who were all about appearing righteous to their peers that they were full of rottenness and dead men's bones, i.e., they stank! This is Christ's righteousness given to us. We are made to be the "righteousness of God": "And be found in him, not having mine own righteousness, which is of the law, but that which is through the faith of Christ, the righteousness which is of God by faith" (Phil. 3:9).

This is the spiritual, supernatural clothing upon that takes place at the moment of salvation that covers us in the sight of God. Notice in the next verse that we "put on Christ"! That is a very important concept that goes totally unnoticed by most readers: "For ye are all the children of God by faith in Christ Jesus. For as many of you as have been baptized into Christ have put on Christ" (Gal. 3:27).

We see this powerful principle demonstrated in the Genesis 27 telling of the story of Jacob and Esau. Esau, who has already sold his birthright to Jacob for a bowl of bean soup, realizes Isaac his father is soon to die. He goes out to hunt a deer to make a savory venison dish for Isaac. Rebecca hears this and instigates a conspiracy with Jacob to cheat Esau out of his paternal blessing as well. After much chicanery, Jacob comes into his father's tent wearing Esau's clothes. Notice what verse 27 says, "And he came near, and kissed him: and he smelled the smell of his raiment, and blessed him, and said, See, the smell of my son is as the smell of a field which the LORD hath blessed" (Gen. 27:27).

Isaac was first tricked by the fact that Rebecca had placed hairy goatskin coverings on his arms and neck. Notice that once again, an animal was sacrificed to make a covering. However, the key point of the story is that Jacob was nearly betrayed by his mouth (a lesson there for all), but it was the aroma of the robe of his brother that sealed the deal! This is such a powerful truth for all of us to remember and walk in: we are not the firstborn (Jesus), but by wearing His robe, with His aroma covering us, we can have the blessing of the firstborn.

Jacob received both the birthright and the blessing by trickery and fraud; we receive them in Christ, not by fraud but as a freely bestowed gift of grace.

> Now then we are ambassadors for Christ, as though God did beseech you by us: we pray you in Christ's stead, be ye reconciled to God. For he hath made him to be sin for us, who knew no sin; that we might be made the righteousness of God in him. (2 Cor. 5:21)

He became the repository of all sin and punishment so that we could receive the fullness of the Father's blessings as a free gift. He has chosen to cloth us in His righteousness to prepare us for a very special role:

> That he might sanctify and cleanse it with the washing of water by the word, That he might present it to himself a glorious church, not having spot, or

wrinkle, or any such thing; but that it should be holy and without blemish. (Eph. 5:25–27)

We are being prepared to be His glorious bride. Once again, we are presented with a description of being clothed in glorious God-given garments.

Let us be glad and rejoice, and give honour to him: for the marriage of the Lamb is come, and his wife hath made herself ready. And to her was granted that she should be arrayed in fine linen, clean and white: for the fine linen is the righteousness of saints. (Rev. 19:7–8)

These verses clearly state that we are granted to wear this garment; it is positively not anything that we have earned or that we deserve to have. It is the righteousness of the saints which comes only and completely through Christ's sacrifice on the cross. It is His sweet aroma that is always pleasing to the Father. In fact, the concept of the sacrifice and the aroma of the smoke from the burning of the sacrifice are so intertwined the Greek words for *sweet aroma* and for *sacrifice* are both derived from the Greek word *thuo*.

Armed with this knowledge, we can walk in confidence knowing that we are wrapped in the robes and the sweet aroma of God's own Son and have been given all blessings and favor of the Father: "Blessed be the God and Father of our Lord Jesus Christ, who hath blessed us with all spiritual blessings in heavenly places in Christ" (Eph. 1:3).

5

The Future

The previous chapter examines the concept that all believers are covered with the robe of Jesus's righteousness, are received by the Father, and are blessed as if they are the firstborn of the Father. As the children of God, we can rest secure that this is his foreknown and foreordained plan: "For whom he did foreknow, he also did predestinate to be conformed to the image of his Son, that he might be the firstborn among many brethren" (Rom. 8:29).

We have the covering of the aroma of Jesus, the firstborn of God. We are covered by His robe of righteousness and by the blood of His sacrifice for our sins. The unbelieving world, on the other hand, has no such covering. Their sins are fully exposed to God's righteous vision and are therefore subject to His full wrath at the uncounted violations of His will and His laws. There will come a day when the wrath of God will be poured out on the world for its sins—first in a measured judgment and later in unmixed fury. When this time comes, we, as believers in Jesus, are in heaven following the rapture and no longer subject to the turmoil coming on the earth during this period of time called the great tribulation. God will then begin to administer His judgment on the unbelieving world. In Revelation 8, we see the first installment of this judgment unfold:

> And another angel came and stood at the altar, having a golden censer; and there was given unto him much incense, that he should offer it with the prayers of all saints upon the golden altar which was before the throne. And the smoke of the incense, which came with the prayers of the saints, ascended up before God out of the angel's hand. And the angel took the censer, and filled it with fire of the altar, and cast it into the earth: and there were voices, and thunderings, and lightnings, and an earthquake. (Rev. 8:3–5)

First, notice that the description of the temple in heaven and its ceremonies looks identical to those prescribed by the law of Moses in the Torah. This is because Moses was shown the heavenly temple by God as a pattern for all he built on earth. All the temple furnishings are identical in design and structure to those he saw during his heavenly visitation with the exception of the ark and the holy of holies as we will see later in this chapter: "And let them make me a sanctuary; that I may dwell among them. According to all that I shew thee, after the pattern of the tabernacle, and the pattern of all the instruments thereof, even so shall ye make it" (Exod. 25:9).

In Revelation 8:3, we see the angel is ministering at the golden altar of incense. He is shown placing "much incense" on the altar. This is in line with the normal temple worship on earth. Here, however, there is a very special ingredient added to the mixture as it is placed on the altar: the "prayers of the saints": "And when he had taken the book, the four beasts and four and twenty elders fell down before the Lamb, having every one of them harps, and golden vials full of odours, which are the prayers of saints" (Rev. 5:8).

It is mentally staggering and extremely humbling to know that God Almighty is "bottling up" all our prayers, imperfect though they usually are, in order to release them in his wrath during the final judgment. Just think of all the prayers of persecuted saints down through the ages that are just waiting to be poured out! On the other hand, try to imagine the prayers beyond number that have been prayed for unsaved loved ones down through time or the prayers prayed by citizens of ungodly nations for mercy to be shown to their land in the face of God's judgment.

> And when he had opened the fifth seal, I saw under the altar the souls of them that were slain for the word of God, and for the testimony which they held: And they cried with a loud voice, saying, How long, O Lord, holy and true, dost thou not judge and avenge our blood on them that dwell on the

earth? And white robes were given unto every one of them; and it was said unto them, that they should rest yet for a little season, until their fellowservants also and their brethren, that should be killed as they were, should be fulfilled. (Rev. 6:10–11)

The smoke from the burning of this mixture of incense and prayer rises up just as on earth; in this scenario, however, there is a slight difference. The place of God's presence in the temple was between the cherubim, above the mercy seat on the ark of the covenant. In the heavenly temple, the place of God's presence and the holy of holies is no less than God's own throne. Revelation 8:4 says that the smoke "ascended up before God out of the angel's hand." The Greek word used here *enopion* literally means "in the eye." Once again, we see the aroma, either good or bad, coming up into His face and stirring him to action, whether to intervene on behalf of his people or to pour out wrath for the actions of rebellious mankind.

In the previous chapters, we see passages describing a sweet aroma rising up before God. Here, we see the total opposite: an enraging smoke of pent up fury and revenge that sets in motion horrific judgments on the sinful men who are destroying the Lord's people and creation. Verse 5 says the angel throws a censor full of coals of fire from the altar, blended incense and prayers, to the earth, and God's judgments begin.

What transpires next in the balance of chapter 8, and into chapter 9, is a series of plagues known as the seven trumpet judgments. These are terrible in nature but are mixed with God's mercy as He tries with very little success to get unbelieving mankind to repent. The set of judgments which follows is simply God's unmixed wrath. These plagues, known as the vial or bowl judgments, are God's final retribution for thousands of years of man's sin and iniquity. The prayers that were burned up with incense in chapter 8 contained not only prayers of vengeance but also many more for mercy on lost humanity and the salvation of men and women. Even in the fiercest trials during the tribulation, Christians will have been interceding for the unsaved. These prayers have by this time been offered on the golden altar, and now all restraint is removed. God now unleashes His full fury:

> And I saw another sign in heaven, great and marvellous, seven angels having the seven last plagues; for in them is filled up the wrath of God… And one of the four beasts gave unto the seven angels seven golden vials full of the wrath of God, who liveth for ever and ever. And the temple was filled with smoke from the glory of God, and from his power; and no man was able to enter into the temple, till the seven plagues of the seven angels were fulfilled… And I heard a great voice out of the temple saying to the seven angels, Go your ways,

and pour out the vials of the wrath of God upon the earth. (Rev. 15:1, 7–8; 16:1)

These "vials" or shallow bowls contain the fullness of God's anger at fallen humanity and are poured out on earth in all their terrible destructiveness. Verse 8 says, "The temple was filled with the smoke of the glory of God." Here, we see the final aroma recorded as filling heaven; God only smells His own righteousness and holiness as He pours out His wrath on the world. His own angels proclaim His justice and justification for these plagues:

> And I heard the angel of the waters say, Thou art righteous, O Lord, which art, and wast, and shalt be, because thou hast judged thus. For they have shed the blood of saints and prophets, and thou hast given them blood to drink; for they are worthy. And I heard another out of the altar say, Even so, Lord God Almighty, true and righteous are thy judgments. (Rev. 16:5–7)

At this point in time, there is no hope left for mankind as God's only response to unregenerate humankind is judgment and wrath. It is our job then to pray and intercede while there is time and opportunity for men to repent and come to a saving knowledge of Jesus Christ. We must send up prayers for our fellow men as a sweet aroma to sooth God's anger at our world's sin and rebellion.

6

Pray without Ceasing

The previous chapter deals with the wrath of God to be revealed during the great tribulation period. With this knowledge comes the realization that the primary reason His wrath is delayed is the prayers of the saints. Without the intercessory prayers of God's people, once again, we find that there is no covering for mankind's sins when God's anger is kindled. Just as the Old Testament priests offered sacrifices that covered them with the odors of incense, blood, and smoke, we today offer the sacrifice of our praises: "By him therefore let us offer the sacrifice of praise to God continually, that is, the fruit of our lips giving thanks to his name" (Heb. 13:15).

The Greek word for *sacrifice* is taken from the word *thuo*, meaning to offer a sacrifice, or more specifically, to burn up a sacrifice. So in praising God and sending up thanksgiving, we are literally making an offering which, like the burning flesh of an animal, covers our sinful human stench.

We saw in the last chapter that these prayers are poured out as an integral part of the plagues on the earth and sinful men. While it is true that there are many prayers of a vengeful nature, it is also true that there are countless prayers offered up to God to withhold His judgment. In fact, God himself invites this type of prayer in one of the most quoted (and prayed) verses of the Old Testament: "If my people, which are called by my name, shall humble themselves, and pray, and seek my face, and turn from their wicked ways; then will I hear from heaven, and will forgive their sin, and will heal their land" (2 Chron. 7:14).

This scripture calls for all God's people, both individually and corporately, to repent and seeks God's forgiveness, healing, and restoration. These prayers are to be made on a personal and a corporate national basis. All throughout the Bible, we find these types of prayers being offered up in an earnest appeal to the Almighty to forgo His wrath. One striking example is found in 1 Samuel 12:

> And Samuel said unto the people, Fear not: ye have done all this wickedness: yet turn not aside from following the LORD, but serve the LORD with all your heart; And turn ye not aside: for then should ye go after vain things, which cannot profit nor deliver; for they are vain. For the LORD will not forsake his people for his great name's sake: because it hath

pleased the LORD to make you his people. Moreover as for me, God forbid that I should sin against the LORD in ceasing to pray for you: but I will teach you the good and the right way: Only fear the LORD, and serve him in truth with all your heart: for consider how great things he hath done for you. But if ye shall still do wickedly, ye shall be consumed, both ye and your king. (1 Sam. 12:20–25)

This absolutely amazing passage is a prophetic precursor to Paul's teachings on grace! Look at the introduction Samuel gives: "fear not: ye have done all this wickedness…" Samuel immediately points out to his listeners that even though they have repeatedly and grievously sinned, they should under no circumstances abandon God as He will not abandon them. They have no reason to be afraid, because God desperately desires to receive them back as penitents and to restore them. He also gives us one of the best and earliest pictures of intercessory prayer: "God forbid that I should sin against the LORD in ceasing to pray for you." Samuel equates failure to pray for his nation and kindred people as a sin against God. Having read this scripture, we should do no less for our families, friends, and neighbors, not to mention our communities, churches, and nation.

In Judges 10, we find an even more frank and brutally honest prayer: "And the children of Israel said unto the LORD, We have sinned: do thou unto us whatsoever seemeth good unto thee; deliver us only, we pray thee, this day" (Judg. 10:15).

What an unbelievably transparent prayer! They fully acknowledge their sin to God and open themselves up to whatever punishment he deems fit. They simply want to return to him and be delivered from the judgments that have come on them. (This is without doubt the best Old Testament equivalent to the Luke 18:13 account of the publican's contrite cry to God: "God be merciful to me a sinner.")

In 1 Kings 8, we find King Solomon taking a more proactive approach: he actually intercedes for his nation and its people ahead of time. He predicts correctly that they will rebel against God in the future and be taken captive into a heathen land. He then proceeds to pray for their forgiveness when and if they repent. All this, even though the sin, captivity, and repentance were centuries in the future.

> If they sin against thee, (for there is no man that sinneth not,) and thou be angry with them, and deliver them to the enemy, so that they carry them away captives unto the land of the enemy, far or near; Yet if they shall bethink themselves in the land whither they were carried captives, and repent, and make supplication unto thee in the land of them that carried them captives, saying, We have sinned, and have done perversely, we have committed

wickedness; And so return unto thee with all their heart, and with all their soul, in the land of their enemies, which led them away captive, and pray unto thee toward their land, which thou gavest unto their fathers, the city which thou hast chosen, and the house which I have built for thy name: Then hear thou their prayer and their supplication in heaven thy dwelling place, and maintain their cause, And forgive thy people that have sinned against thee, and all their transgressions wherein they have transgressed against thee, and give them compassion before them who carried them captive, that they may have compassion on them: For they be thy people, and thine inheritance. (1 Kings 8:46–51)

The apostle Paul doesn't intercede in advance like King Solomon. He simply warns his disciples what is coming in the future and tells them uncategorically that they are the agency whereby the enemy's power and destructive influence are being held back:

> Let no man deceive you by any means: for that day shall not come, except there come a falling away first, and that man of sin be revealed, the son of perdition; Who opposeth and exalteth himself above all that is called God, or that is worshipped; so that he as God sitteth in the temple of God, shewing himself that he is God. Remember ye not, that, when I was yet with you, I told you these things? And now ye

know what withholdeth that he might be revealed in his time. For the mystery of iniquity doth already work: only he who now letteth will let, until he be taken out of the way. And then shall that Wicked be revealed, whom the Lord shall consume with the spirit of his mouth, and shall destroy with the brightness of his coming. (2 Thess. 2:3–8)

Notice verse 7: "he who letteth will let." The Greek word translated "letteth" is *katecho*, meaning literally to hold against. It means, in this context, to restrain or hold back. The "he" is undoubtedly the Spirit and His presence in the church, the body of Christ. We as believers have within us the power of Almighty God in the person of the Holy Spirit. That power will withhold and restrain Satan from doing all he would, especially when we employ our weapon of prayer. The church is standing in the gap as a spiritual covering for the whole world, restraining God's judgment and hindering Satan's activities.

As chapter 1 points out, Acts 10:4 shows us God himself telling Cornelius in a vision that his "prayers and alms are come up for a memorial before God." Once again, we see an example of the sweet aroma of prayer and sacrificial giving being a covering to an otherwise unworthy person. Cornelius was a Gentile and from a Jewish standpoint had no hope. However, his almsgiving and prayers had created a spiritual smoke screen that allowed God to intervene in his situation sending the apostle Peter to preach the Gospel, resulting in salvation for Cornelius's whole family and household.

When Paul writes his first letter to Timothy, who was a newly installed bishop/pastor, he gives him a very plain, simple, and straightforward assignment: "I exhort therefore, that, first of all, supplications, prayers, intercessions, and giving of thanks, be made for all men" (1 Tim. 2:1).

It was Timothy's job, and ours, to make all kinds of prayer for "all men." No effort should be spared to provide the spiritual aroma that sooths God's anger and prolongs His mercy on our loved ones, our churches, our nation, and our world. His admonition to the church at Thessalonica was even more simple and pointed: "Pray without ceasing" (1 Thess. 5:17).

7

Enter the Temple

The previous chapter explains in detail the concept of our prayers producing a spiritual covering much as the physical smells of an animal sacrifice did during the Old Testament era. In this chapter, that idea will be taken further to demonstrate our ability to enter into holy places spiritually with the covering of a "sweet aroma" we have been provided. We can and should enter God's presence just as the Old Testament priests did—one step at a time in prayers and thanksgiving. We are already covered with the robe of Jesus's righteousness and should be covered in the sweet aroma of His blood and our praise.

> But Christ being come an high priest of good things to come, by a greater and more perfect tabernacle, not made with hands, that is to say, not of this building; Neither by the blood of goats and calves,

but by his own blood he entered in once into the holy place, having obtained eternal redemption for us. (Heb. 9:11–12)

As this passage plainly says, we no longer enter by the blood of animal sacrifices but by Jesus's blood and the finished work of the cross. It also states that He entered once into the holy of holies to offer one sacrifice, His own body and blood, once and for all. He was 100 percent righteous and we were 100 percent sinful, yet He bore all our sins to give us His righteousness: "For he hath made him to be sin for us, who knew no sin; that we might be made the righteousness of God in him" (2 Cor. 5:21).

This is how we can have His robe and His smell when approaching the Father. We can enter the temple of God spiritually with assurance that we will be received just as if we were His firstborn son, because we are wearing His robe and carrying His sweet aroma of a perfect sacrifice: "In whom we have boldness and access with confidence by the faith of him (Jesus)" (Eph. 3:12).

The nation of Israel as a whole, and the Pharisees specifically, by contrast were attempting to please God through their own efforts. They failed to realize or recognize how utterly futile these efforts were. Paul declares this truth in Romans 10, stating that they "had a zeal…not according to knowledge."

> Brethren, my heart's desire and prayer to God for Israel is, that they might be saved. For I bear them record that they have a zeal of God, but not according to knowledge. For they being ignorant of God's righteousness, and going about to establish their own righteousness, have not submitted themselves unto the righteousness of God. (Rom. 10:1–3)

They failed to understand that their righteousness would never be sufficient to fulfill God's demands of holy perfection. God can countenance absolutely no sin in, or entering into, His presence, and therefore all human efforts are doomed to failure. Jesus targets the Pharisees in particular on this account, repeatedly chastising them for their pseudo-spiritual hypocrisy: "For I say unto you, That except your righteousness shall exceed the righteousness of the scribes and Pharisees, ye shall in no case enter into the kingdom of heaven" (Matt. 5:20).

He not only tells the crowd that the scribes and Pharisees are not righteous but states that unless they possess a form of righteousness far superior to theirs (i.e., his righteousness), they will never even enter the kingdom! He likens the scribes and Pharisees to graves and says they are full of rottenness:

> Woe unto you, scribes and Pharisees, hypocrites! for ye are like unto whited sepulchres, which indeed appear beautiful outward, but are within full of dead

> men's bones, and of all uncleanness. Even so ye also outwardly appear righteous unto men, but within ye are full of hypocrisy and iniquity. (Matt. 23:27–28)

This sounds awful to us as Westerners, but to a Middle Eastern person at the time of Christ, this had an entirely different and far worse meaning. The difference hinges on the understanding of the grave or sepulchre. In those days, a corpse was placed temporarily in a grave for the period of time necessary for the body to decay. This was for the purpose of promoting the rapid decomposition of the body. The combination of heat and bacterial action accomplished this in a relatively short time, usually a few months. When the flesh was fully gone, the dried bones were then placed in a bone box called an ossuary and placed in a permanent family tomb. Thus, when Jesus said they were "within full of dead men's bones, and of all uncleanness," they would have taken this as an enormous insult based on the fact that merely being in proximity to a dead body made you ceremonially unclean. Now Jesus is saying that their lives were the spiritual equivalent of rotting corpses in God's eyes. In fact, he was telling them bluntly: "you may be trying to look good on the outside but in reality, you stink horribly to God!"

Once again, we have the representation of mankind's fallen sinfulness as a stench to the Lord. This gives a far deeper and more profound meaning to the scriptures concerning baptism:

> Know ye not, that so many of us as were baptized into Jesus Christ were baptized into his death? Therefore we are buried with him by baptism into death: that like as Christ was raised up from the dead by the glory of the Father, even so we also should walk in newness of life. For if we have been planted together in the likeness of his death, we shall be also in the likeness of his resurrection: Knowing this, that our old man is crucified with him, that the body of sin might be destroyed, that henceforth we should not serve sin. (Rom. 6:3–6).

If sinful, hypocritical men are characterized as having the smell of dead, decaying bodies spiritually, then how much more importance does this layer onto the act of believer's baptism? Peter puts it even more bluntly in his first epistle: "The like figure whereunto even baptism doth also now save us (not the putting away of the filth of the flesh, but the answer of a good conscience toward God,) by the resurrection of Jesus Christ" (1 Pet. 3:21).

He calls the old man the "filth of the flesh." How much more urgency is demanded to publicly denounce the old man and the fleshly life by the symbolic burial of baptism! In Jesus's time, many religious Jews were baptized every day as a symbolic washing and a renewing of their commitment to God. They felt that it was a baptism into their future. Paul tells us in Hebrews that although these things aren't wrong in and of themselves, the new covenant in Christ is far superior.

> The Holy Ghost this signifying, that the way into the holiest of all was not yet made manifest, while as the first tabernacle was yet standing: Which was a figure for the time then present, in which were offered both gifts and sacrifices, that could not make him that did the service perfect, as pertaining to the conscience; Which stood only in meats and drinks, and divers washings, and carnal ordinances, imposed on them until the time of reformation. But Christ being come an high priest of good things to come…(Heb. 9:8–11)

This leaves us with an inescapable point: if these physical washings and baptisms had such an important role as symbolic and prophetic forerunners in the old covenant, how much more the spiritual realities of the revelation of those symbols and allegories in the new.

> As Christ also loved the church, and gave himself for it; That he might sanctify and cleanse it with the washing of water by the word, That he might present it to himself a glorious church, not having spot, or wrinkle, or any such thing; but that it should be holy and without blemish. (Eph 5:26–27).

The Father wants to cleanse each of us individually and all of us collectively in order to make us into a sanctified, spotless bride for Christ.

8

Get Dressed

In all this discussion, we have concentrated on the things that God smells and what aromas we as believers have, or conversely, which ones we need to avoid. In this chapter, I want to focus on what we need to do to prepare ourselves to enhance our spiritual aroma. This chapter centers first of all on our getting dressed up so as to smell our very best before the Father. As chapter 4 points out, we have a garment of salvation and a robe of righteousness (Isa. 61:10) that are provided by Christ when we give our life to Him. These are automatically ours and neither require nor involve any effort on our part. However, no soldier would go into battle dressed in only a robe. We are admonished by Paul to get armored up in preparation for the spiritual warfare that will surely come to every born-again believer.

> Finally, my brethren, be strong in the Lord, and in the power of his might. Put on the whole armour of God, that ye may be able to stand against the wiles of the devil. For we wrestle not against flesh and blood, but against principalities, against powers, against the rulers of the darkness of this world, against spiritual wickedness in high places. Wherefore take unto you the whole armour of God, that ye may be able to withstand in the evil day, and having done all, to stand. Stand therefore, having your loins girt about with truth, and having on the breastplate of righteousness; And your feet shod with the preparation of the gospel of peace; Above all, taking the shield of faith, wherewith ye shall be able to quench all the fiery darts of the wicked. And take the helmet of salvation, and the sword of the Spirit, which is the word of God. (Eph. 6:10–17)

In this passage, there are six pieces of armor mentioned. Each and every one serves a specific purpose in our Christian walk and warfare. In 1 Samuel 17, we read that King Saul outfitted David in his armor, but David refused because he had not "proved it." That is to say David had not fought in it and he knew it was given to him only because of Saul's doubt and unbelief. Saul quite obviously didn't think David would be able to stand up to Goliath, so he wanted to "help God out" a little. In contrast, our spiritual armor is given by God and is given because of our faith and belief.

God not only provides the armor, but He empowers it and us to fight effectively and successfully. Notice also that it is called the "armour of God." It's not our armor but God's armor. It has been tried by none other than Jesus himself. Luke 4 records the battle of temptation between Satan and Jesus. Once again, we see the principle of smelling like the firstborn. We not only have on his robe of righteousness, but we also have his armor available to us.

We have aromas surrounding us that are associated with the armor as well. The leather harness work and strapping of Bible times armor would have been rubbed with oil regularly to keep it pliable. The shield would have been soaked in a solution of alum and water. This solution absorbs oxygen when heated, so it acts as a natural fire-retardant to "quench" the fiery darts (flaming arrows). Just as in our approach to God in worship, we have a covering of a pleasing aroma when entering battle.

Another step in our getting dressed is to be clothed upon and empowered by the Holy Spirit. Jesus admonished His disciples to stay at Jerusalem, i.e., to not start their ministry until they were clothed upon with God's power in the person of the Holy Spirit: "And, behold, I send the promise of my Father upon you: but tarry ye in the city of Jerusalem, until ye be endued (clothed) with power from on high" (Luke 24:49).

This was accomplished on the day of Pentecost when all the disciples were filled with the Holy Spirit in the upper room. These disciples who had been cowering in the upper room in fear for their very lives are now seen running boldly into the streets of Jerusalem, preaching Jesus without the slightest hesitation or nervousness.

> And when the day of Pentecost was fully come, they were all with one accord in one place. And suddenly there came a sound from heaven as of a rushing mighty wind, and it filled all the house where they were sitting. And there appeared unto them cloven tongues like as of fire, and it sat upon each of them. And they were all filled with the Holy Ghost, and began to speak with other tongues, as the Spirit gave them utterance. And there were dwelling at Jerusalem Jews, devout men, out of every nation under heaven. Now when this was noised abroad, the multitude came together, and were confounded, because that every man heard them speak in his own language. And they were all amazed and marvelled, saying one to another, Behold, are not all these which speak Galileans? And how hear we every man in our own tongue, wherein we were born?...we do hear them speak in our tongues the wonderful works of God. And they were all amazed, and were in doubt, saying one to another, What meaneth this? Others mocking said, These men are full of new wine. But Peter, standing up with the eleven, lifted up his voice, and said unto them, Ye men of Judaea, and all ye that dwell at Jerusalem, be this known unto you, and hearken to my words:

> For these are not drunken, as ye suppose, seeing it is but the third hour of the day. But this is that which was spoken by the prophet Joel; And it shall come to pass in the last days, saith God, I will pour out of my Spirit upon all flesh…(Acts 2:1–17)

The mention of fire is very significant in this passage. In fact, this same idea was prophesied concerning Jesus:

> Behold my servant, whom I uphold; mine elect, in whom my soul delighteth; I have put my spirit upon him: he shall bring forth judgment to the Gentiles. He shall not cry, nor lift up, nor cause his voice to be heard in the street. A bruised reed shall he not break, and the smoking flax shall he not quench: he shall bring forth judgment unto truth. (Isa. 42:1–3)

Let's examine the phrase *smoking flax*. The oil lamps commonly used in that day would have had a wick of braided or spun flax. In Acts 2:3, the disciples are described as having "tongues or flames of fire resting on them." A flame being emitted by an oil lamp means that the lamp has a supply of olive oil in it. A smoking flax denotes a lamp that is low on oil or even empty. The wick is dry and is actually burning itself. Here again is an odor: a burning wick stinks! A wick that is well soaked has only the pleasant odor of burning oil. The oil is heated by the flame and is vaporized. The aerosol oil then burns, and the wick is left untouched. This speaks to the fact that when we are filled with, and walking in, the Holy Spirit, it is all by His power and we have no part in the powerful spiritual life He provides. Little wonder that Jesus stated first that He was the "light of the world" and then later says "ye are the light of the world." This denotes this same transfer of power and anointing to His followers: "The spirit of man is the candle (lamp) of the LORD, searching all the inward parts of the belly" (Prov. 20:27).

We are simply a vessel that holds this precious "oil." We have within our spirit man a capacity for God to fill us with His holy anointing, to be a light in a dark world: "For thou art my lamp, O LORD: and the LORD will lighten my darkness" (2 Sam. 22:29).

These principles give a deep additional significance to the parable of the ten virgins found in Matthew 25:

> Then shall the kingdom of heaven be likened unto ten virgins, which took their lamps, and went forth to meet the bridegroom. And five of them were wise, and five were foolish. They that were foolish took their lamps, and took no oil with them: But the wise took oil in their vessels with their lamps. While the bridegroom tarried, they all slumbered and slept. And at midnight there was a cry made, Behold, the bridegroom cometh; go ye out to meet him. Then all those virgins arose, and trimmed their lamps. And the foolish said unto the wise, Give us of your oil; for our lamps are gone out. (Matt. 25:1–8)

The tense of the Greek word translated "gone out" should really be rendered "going out." The principle of the dry wick comes into play once again in this passage. They "took their lamps, and took no oil." Just as these "foolish" individuals, we can operate without the filling and empowering of the Spirit, but sooner or later, our lamp will falter and fail to give out its light. We will give off the stench of a burning wick. We need to be filled and refilled continually and consistently with the oil of the Holy Spirit.

9

The Prodigal

The blessing of the firstborn comes upon us as a result of being in covenant with the Father. It is a family covenant. We are blessed because He chose to adopt us as His children and enter into covenant with us. All the inheritance by rights belongs to the firstborn, but Jesus, in obedience to His Father, chose to share it with us.

> For ye have not received the spirit of bondage again to fear; but ye have received the Spirit of adoption, whereby we cry, Abba, Father. The Spirit itself beareth witness with our spirit, that we are the children of God: And if children, then heirs; heirs of God, and joint-heirs with Christ. (Rom. 8:15–17)

God wants us to walk in the abundance of His blessings. He has made every effort to bring us into the place where

His favor is: "He that spared not his own Son, but delivered him up for us all, how shall he not with him also freely give us all things?" (Rom. 8:32).

Even though we do not deserve these blessings, God makes them available as free gifts. We, on the other hand, tend to take them for granted and treat a loving Father as a sort of divine Santa Claus. We long for the gifts rather than the presence of the giver. This almost inevitably leads to a prodigal spirit. We receive His unmerited gifts and then walk away to live independent of His will. In Luke 15, Jesus uses this parable to teach us concerning this syndrome:

> And he said, A certain man had two sons: And the younger of them said to his father, Father, give me the portion of goods that falleth to me. And he divided unto them his living. And not many days after the younger son gathered all together, and took his journey into a far country, and there wasted his substance with riotous living. And when he had spent all, there arose a mighty famine in that land; and he began to be in want. And he went and joined himself to a citizen of that country; and he sent him into his fields to feed swine. And he would fain have filled his belly with the husks that the swine did eat: and no man gave unto him. And when he came to himself, he said, How many hired servants of my father's have bread enough and to spare, and I perish with hunger! I will arise and go to my father, and will say unto him, Father, I have sinned against

heaven, and before thee, And am no more worthy to be called thy son: make me as one of thy hired servants. And he arose, and came to his father. But when he was yet a great way off, his father saw him, and had compassion, and ran, and fell on his neck, and kissed him. And the son said unto him, Father, I have sinned against heaven, and in thy sight, and am no more worthy to be called thy son. But the father said to his servants, Bring forth the best robe, and put it on him; and put a ring on his hand, and shoes on his feet: And bring hither the fatted calf, and kill it; and let us eat, and be merry: For this my son was dead, and is alive again; he was lost, and is found. And they began to be merry. (Luke 15:11–25)

The younger son, who represents believers, rejects his father's authority and wants only his material blessings. He walks away from the center of his prosperity and blessings contrary to his own best interests and goes to live a rebellious lifestyle. This leads to poverty and lack. How like ourselves as Christians: we many times only want God involved in our life when we have a serious need that we can't fill within our own abilities. This young man after a season of pleasure finds himself in a very degraded condition and finally comes to his senses: "I will arise and go to my father." It is a good and sensible choice, but look at the condition he comes to before making it. He has been living among and eating with a herd of swine. He was no doubt filthy in the extreme, and his odor must have been unbearable. He travels the long dirt road home in Middle Eastern heat, only to become even more offensive than he already was; now he is filthy, smelly, dusty, and sweaty. None of this registers with his loving father who sees him coming from a distance (did he perhaps smell him coming?) and responds, not with condemnation or repulsion but with love and compassion. Notice his first command to the servants: "bring the best robe." Since the inheritance belonged to the eldest son, the firstborn, the "best robe" by rights belonged to him! Once again, we are presented with the picture of ourselves being arrayed with the robe (and the aroma) of the firstborn. The prodigal is supplied with a covering that hides his uncleanness.

We like the prodigal have a need that we cannot fill, and yet God freely gives us a supply that we are so undeserving of. This is the definition of grace: undeserved, unmerited favor and blessing. When we are at our filthiest and smelliest, God doesn't perceive our wretched condition; He merely sees and smells the righteousness and sweet aroma of Jesus. Unlike the eldest son in the parable, however, Jesus has no jealousy toward us. He freely gives all to us because he loves his creation, especially the pinnacle of his creation: mankind.

When Adam was created and placed in the garden, he was given a divine commission. God made him the gardener over all His creation: "And the LORD God took the man, and put him into the garden of Eden to dress it and to keep it" (Gen. 2:15).

The word translated "dress" means to serve or labor, but it also has a connotation of worshipping. Man was intended to worship and serve God through being His agent in the earth. The word rendered "keep" means to watch over or guard. He was empowered by God and arrayed in a covering of the glory of God. He was naked but was unaware because of this covering. When he and Eve rebelled against the Lord and fell into sin, they were aware that they were naked. Why? Because their spiritual covering was gone.

Now look forward in time to Jesus's resurrection. When Jesus arose from the grave, the disciples found the graveclothes still in the grave: "Then cometh Simon Peter following him, and went into the sepulchre, and seeth the linen clothes lie, And the napkin, that was about his head, not lying with the linen clothes, but wrapped together in a place by itself" (John 20:6–7).

When Jesus was later seen by Mary Magdalene, she thought he was the gardener.

> But Mary stood without at the sepulchre weeping: and as she wept, she stooped down, and looked into the sepulchre, And seeth two angels in white sitting, the one at the head, and the other at the feet, where the body of Jesus had lain. And they say unto her, Woman, why weepest thou? She saith unto them,

> Because they have taken away my Lord, and I know not where they have laid him. And when she had thus said, she turned herself back, and saw Jesus standing, and knew not that it was Jesus. Jesus saith unto her, Woman, why weepest thou? whom seekest thou? She, supposing him to be the gardener, saith unto him, Sir, if thou have borne him hence, tell me where thou hast laid him, and I will take him away. (John 20:12–16)

What was Jesus wearing for Mary to think He was the gardener? From the fact that the graveclothes were still in the tomb, he obviously wasn't wearing them. The Roman soldiers gambled for his robe and other clothing at the foot of the cross. So what was he wearing? Could Jesus have come out of the grave wearing the same covering of glory Adam lost? He is called in 1 Corinthians 15 the "last Adam"!

> And so it is written, The first man Adam was made a living soul; the last Adam was made a quickening spirit. Howbeit that was not first which is spiritual, but that which is natural; and afterward that which is spiritual. The first man is of the earth, earthy: the second man is the Lord from heaven. (1 Cor. 15:45–47)

We are believers and yet we are so often like the prodigal. We have so much available to us, yet we often live in the pig pen spiritually. Despite all our failings, we get to someday wear a glory suit like Jesus's. Even Adam had no such covering before the fall. When, as 1 Corinthians 15:53 says, "this mortal must put on immortality," we will have truly become all the Father planned and wills for us to be. Until then, we wear the firstborn's robe and give off a sweet aroma that rises up before the Father: "Beloved, now are we the sons of God, and it doth not yet appear what we shall be: but we know that, when he shall appear, we shall be like him; for we shall see him as he is" (1 John 3:2).

Appendix A

Prayers

The following is a compilation of prayers which will allow the reader to begin or build a relationship with the Lord. These are not a "formula" but a template. Your own problems, prayers, and petitions need to be molded into them.

Prayer for salvation:

Heavenly Father, I come to you today, acknowledging the fact that I have lived my life independent of you. I have fallen far short of your standards, which the Bible calls sin. I repent and turn from my sin and ask for your forgiveness. I know that your son, Jesus, died for my sins and was resurrected. I believe on Him and ask Him to be my Savior and Lord. I thank you for your free gift of salvation. In Jesus's name, Amen.

Prayer for the fruit of the Spirit:

Father, I know that Your ways are as far above my ways as the heavens are above the earth. I need Your help to change and become more like Christ in my thoughts, attitudes, and actions. Transform me by your Holy Spirit and produce in me the spiritual fruit of love, joy, peace, patience, kindness, goodness, faithfulness, gentleness, and self-control. Make all my life a testimony of your power to change. In Jesus's name, Amen.

Prayer for the baptism of the Spirit:

Heavenly Father, I come to you laying self and self will on the altar of sacrifice and submitting myself to the washing of the water of your Word. By an act of my will, I crucify the flesh, I empty myself of me, and I ask you to fill me and baptize me in your Holy Spirit. I believe I receive according to Mark 11 and I thank you for the gift of the Holy Spirit. In Jesus's name, Amen.

Prayer of dedication and consecration:

Heavenly Father, I dedicate myself to the pursuit of your presence and life-changing power. I consecrate myself to you. Make me an instrument suitable for your service. Remove from me everything that is not in line with your will and plans. Create in me every ability, gift, and talent needed to accomplish your eternal purposes in my life. I surrender myself to you. In Jesus's name, Amen.

Prayer for clothing:

Savior, I come to you now thanking you for your suffering and death on the cross for my sin, allowing me clothed with salvation according 2 Chronicles 6:41. I now ask that you wrap me in the robe of your righteousness so that I truly give off your fragrance and receive the blessing of the firstborn in all I put my hand to. In Jesus's name, Amen.

Appendix B

Prayers for "Entering In"

The following is a compilation of prayers for entering in taken from my book *Into His Presence*.

Prayer for entrance into the Tabernacle:

"Our Father who is in heaven, Hallowed be Your name," I enter the Tabernacle of your presence with thankfulness. Thank you for Your many and great blessings. Thank you for Your free gift of salvation in your son, Jesus Christ. For all your supply and blessings which were accomplished and provided by the finished work of the cross, I thank you and I praise you. I magnify and declare holy your great name, for you are worthy of all worship and honor and glory and power and blessing and praise forever. In Jesus's name, Amen.

Prayer for cleansing at the laver:

Heavenly Father, your kingdom come in my life, in my will, in my attitudes, and in my behavior. Cleanse me of all sins, worldly distractions, and thoughts patterns. Create in me a clean heart and a mind centered on you alone as I come into this time of prayer and fellowship with you. Sanctify me as a vessel fit for your service and worship. In Jesus's name, Amen.

Prayer for cleansing at the altar:

Father, "Your will be done" in every part of my life, my thought processes, my attitudes, and my Christian walk. Right now, by an act of my will, I lay myself on your altar as a living sacrifice. I crucify my flesh according to Galatians 2:20 that no longer will it be me that lives but Christ who lives in me. I put myself in submission to your will and in obedience to your Word, so that I can worship you and serve others. Prepare me to enter into your holy place. In Jesus's name. Amen.

Prayer for abiding at the table of bread:

Lord, give me this day my daily bread, the bread of life that proceeds only from you. Help me to be in a perpetual state of prayer and meditation on you and Your Word. Create in me a thankful heart that is always set on praising and worshipping you. Change me in your glorious presence. In Jesus's name, Amen.

Prayer for standing before the menorah:

Father God, I come to you with open arms and heart. I stand before the light of your Word and invite you to search me and try me. Show me the areas of my life, attitudes, actions, and thought processes that don't meet your standard. Forgive me my debts, my sins against you. Give me strength so that I, by an act of my will, can give forgiveness. Purge out of me everything that hinders our fellowship so that Your light can shine through me more clearly in a dark and fallen world. In Jesus's name, Amen.

Prayer for worship at the altar of incense:

"Lead me not into temptation but deliver me from evil" is my prayer today so that I can avoid the snares of the enemy and follow you more closely. I thank you that you hear my prayers. I submit my will to yours and I worship you for all you have done and continue to do in my life. I lift my petitions to you for _____
and I believe that I have received. In Jesus's name, Amen.

Prayer for entering in the holy of holies:

Heavenly Father, give me the faith, commitment, and humility to press in to the holy of holies. I recognize that only through the blood of Jesus do I have access to your presence, your favor, and your covenants. I come into your holy presence with praise and worship as Jesus taught us: "For Yours is the kingdom and the power and the glory forever." Your Word says that if I abide in Christ, all my petitions will be granted, but I come now in adoration, seeking your face and not your hands. I pray according to 2 Corinthians 3:18 that I will be changed by beholding your glory into the same image, the image of Christ. In Jesus's name, Amen.

www.ingramcontent.com/pod-product-compliance
Lightning Source LLC
Chambersburg PA
CBHW070550300426
44113CB00011B/1845